STRESS AND RECOVERY

About the pamphlet:

This pamphlet explores the stress factors common to a recovering lifestyle, and outlines ways to deal with stress and to make it a positive force.

About the author:

Patricia Hoolihan has spent several years working with adolescents in the field of chemical dependency, prevention, and aftercare. She is currently working on her Master's Degree at the University of Minnesota.

STRESS AND RECOVERY

PATRICIA HOOLIHAN

HAZELDEN®

First published August, 1984.

Copyright © 1984, Hazelden Foundation.
All rights reserved. No portion of this publication may be reproduced in any manner without the written permission of the publisher.

ISBN: 0-89486-236-7

Printed in the United States of America.

Introduction

There is no such thing as a stress-free life, so before we throw up our hands in surrender, let's remind ourselves that stress performs an important function in our lives.

For example, when an animal runs in front of our car, it is the stress alarm system in our bodies that gives us the ability to react with the necessary speed. The body is stressed as the heart rate speeds up and adrenalin pumps through the system, allowing reflexes to be sharper than usual. So we brake in time to miss the animal, without endangering ourselves or other cars on the road. A little further down the road we find ourselves breathing deeply, our body muscles warm with relief. After the emergency is dealt with there is usually a period of deeper than usual calm before the body returns to its normal level of function.

There is a great deal to be learned from this natural physiological process. In the following pages, we are going to look at applying that natural wisdom to the more long-term stress problems in our lives.

It would be nice if all the stress in our lives were as easy to see or tangible to deal with as the example just given. However, most of the stress in our lives is not that simple. As recovering people, we are constantly dealing with changes in our lives. There seems to be a cyclical relationship between change and stress.

When a situation becomes stressful enough in our lives, we will seek ways to change it. Take, for instance, Anna, single, in her late twenties. For years her drinking had progressed, making her more and more of a loner. She often preferred to return home alone after work rather than socialize with her friends. At home she could drink wine and read her books with no one to keep track of how much she drank. On the few occasions she did socialize with her friends, she found herself increasingly alone in the midst of the crowd: alone with her bottle of wine.

She began to worry about herself. Her uneasiness with other people made life more and more uncomfortable for her. The stress of her isolation and uneasiness eventually brought Anna to seek help from a woman counselor. She focused on her loneliness, but with the help of her astute counselor she soon found herself in treatment for her alcoholism.

In the beginning, Anna may have used alcohol to numb herself to stressful events or realities in her life. However, as alcohol became more crucial to her, the use of it created its own stress, adding to that which she already felt. When this reached a crisis point she sought assistance. She began to face her problem and made the decision to stop drinking, with a lot of help. This major life change, of course, was stressful in and of itself. Her recovery continues to create new challenges, so Anna continues to encounter stress that is part of growing.

So we begin to see the cyclical relationship between change and stress. Stressful events can be a wonderful motivator, causing us to make positive changes. The changes themselves create stress, for we are creatures of habit and appear to have a natural resistance to change. It seems that an important part of recovery is finding the balance in our own lives. We need some stress to keep us stimulated, challenged, and growing. Too much stress robs us of the ability to enjoy life — it has a destructive effect on our physical health and our relationships. Stress can be compared to the tension of a violin string — we need "enough tension to make music, but not so much that it snaps."[1]

Each of us needs to find our own individual balance. In this pamphlet we will focus on ways to find that balance in the midst of the stress factors that are common to a recovering lifestyle. We will look at ways to honor the stress that is a part of growing, and ways to avoid being ruled by an overload of stress.

---

[1]Dr. Donald Tubesing, *Kicking Your Stress Habits* (Duluth, MN, Whole Person Associates).

Reentry Stress

We have already seen an example of stress in the life of a nonrecovering person. Since this pamphlet is primarily for those of us recovering from alcohol or other drug dependency, let's look at the role of stress in recovery.

Whether or not we go through treatment, there is the initial major revelation for all of us when we admit we are powerless over our chemical. The decision to stop using our chemical creates a major life change. In some way, our vision of life is forever changed. It's like pulling up a shade in the morning. We can no longer live in the darkness of our delusion. Light falls in upon our life in a new way, no longer shielded by our chemical, nor by our delusionary control.

When the sun first shines in, our eyes blink at the brightness. It takes time for our eyes, indeed for our bodies and souls, to adjust to our new vision. Whether we first pull up the shades of our delusions in a treatment program or in A.A., we feel bonded to those with whom we share those important first moments of light. The change is profound and affects us in every way — emotionally, physically, spiritually. While we are in treatment or in our meetings, we are surrounded by people who understand that change.

There comes a time for each of us, however, to step back into our families and the rest of our daily lives. This can be difficult. People in the rest of our lives may not understand what we have been through. In fact, they have grown used to dealing with our old alcoholic selves and it will take some time and some rough spots for everyone to learn to deal with our sobriety.

Let's call this reentry stress. Think of how hard it is to come back from a vacation. We have just spent a number of days in a somewhat insulated environment, surrounded by family or friends, with very few distractions. The transition from an intense, focused experience back to daily life is often a stressful one. We go through reentry stress the same way astronauts do when they reenter the earth's atmosphere.

It's important to know that the transition back into daily life is difficult. Talking about it with others who understand is helpful. Carrying the burden alone is an added, unnecessary stress.

Just as astronauts take time to allow their bodies to recover, this is a time when we need to be easy on ourselves. We must understand that our sober lifestyle is a process — we don't have to do it all at once. Taking it a day at a time is essential, as is acknowledging and talking about the changes that are happening. It is also important to balance the intensity of these changes with some relaxation.

This takes us back to the example of how our bodies react to an emergency. When the emergency is over, the body enters a deep calm. We need to create this balance in our lives, like the rhythm of the tides. As we return to our lives as sober human beings, let's give ourselves time to recover. Let's take time to do whatever it is that most relaxes us. Anything from skiing to sunbathing will work — the most important thing is that it calms and relaxes us. Learning how this individual balance works for us will help keep stress at a manageable level.

Some of us expect a lot of ourselves right away. We need to remember that adapting ourselves to a chemical-free life takes time and is done a little bit each day. It is helpful to not take on very many changes at one time.

Changing Relationships

Often both the recovering person and his or her family fall prey to the myth that, now that the chemical has been removed, everything will improve immediately. We forget that we spent all those years adapting to the use of the chemical and its effects and now it is gone. It is an adjustment for all of us, one we will work on for a long time.

One recovering teenager has said about her mother, "I don't understand. She wanted me to quit drinking and now that I have, she's not any happier."

This is not uncommon. Feelings we could hide from in our intoxication now surface. We need to learn new ways to relate to our friends and family. Many of us feel like beginners, young birds just learning to fly. We are learning how to be honest, responsible, sober adults, and for many of us, this means learning new behaviors. The small bird folds up at night, exhausted from beating its wings to learn to fly. So do we feel the stress in our lives as we beat our wings trying out new behaviors.

Take for instance, Bruce, a forty-year-old executive. As he learns to live a sober life, one of the things he realizes is that, between his drinking and his business, he has really neglected spending time with his two children.

First of all there is the pain for him of seeing his neglect and feeling his remorse about it. This is stressful in and of itself. Then, as he begins to do something about it, he is awkward at first. He has to learn how to arrange his schedule to include his children. He discovers that, in some ways, they are strangers to one another. The first few times he takes them out or plays with them, he hardly knows what to say.

The awkwardness of these new behaviors is stressful. It is difficult to break patterns we have been living with for years. This kind of stress is a part of making changes. We can take heart from the young bird who does learn to fly, eventually, with grace and ease.

As Bruce spends time with his children, he learns how to be with them and talk with them. He becomes less a stranger and more the father they always wanted. Although it may not happen immediately, in the long run Bruce will feel better about himself for having learned, even at a later age, how to be a better father. It is never too late for healing to happen, especially within a family. The stress involved in making these changes is worthwhile. It is part of learning to be more fully human.

It is helpful for people like Bruce to talk about the awkwardness while going through it. This eases the added stress of feeling all alone with it. Hearing from others who have gone through the same process helps give hope and comfort. Talking about the difficulties of new behaviors helps keep the stress level manageable.

To pretend that the change from a using lifestyle to a nonusing one is simple or easy adds the considerable stress of expecting ourselves to be superhuman. Let's remind ourselves of a line from that wise prayer, *Desiderata:* "Be gentle with yourself."

There will be enough stresses along with the growing we do as recovering human beings. We do not need to add to that by expecting to change with a speed and thoroughness that is beyond our human limits.

Peer pressure is another stressful factor most of us will encounter as we return to our daily lives and continue to choose not to use.

This is especially difficult for adolescents. They return to a culture full of experimentation with chemicals. There is a lot of pressure to "be cool," to belong. It is important to acknowledge the difficulty of this situation. Young people desperately need support from others like them and from people who care about them. They need to find ways to reinforce their sober lifestyle.

At any age we encounter some of this peer pressure. Perhaps it comes from friends at work whom we once used with. It may come from our own family of origin, where people are used to a long history of drinking together. This pressure is difficult to deal with, especially when we are newly sober. We need to rely on the help of our program and our group members to support us through this kind of stressful encounter.

Changing Our Own Behavior

When we doubt the power of habit, all we need to do is try putting on our coats with the opposite arm first, rather than how we usually do it. It will feel awkward and clumsy. It may be the first time we are aware we had a specific and habitual way of putting on our coats.

As newly sober people, our efforts to be more honest and responsible are often awkward and clumsy. Carol, a recovering housewife, realizes she never learned how to directly tell her husband when she was angry with him. Part of her recovery is learning how to do this, but at first it is scary for her. She trips over her words, doesn't always pick the best times to do it, and finds herself vacillating between extremes.

The stress this awkwardness creates is a natural part of changing old patterns and creating new ones. It is often frustrating, and we need to be patient with ourselves. Like any new skill, it requires practice, and we will make mistakes. An adult taking her first piano lesson would expect to spend a long time practicing scales and fingering. We need that same kind of patience with learning new behaviors. Just like the scales on the piano, the new behaviors will become less stressful and far more rewarding than our old dishonest and hiding ways.

For Carol, it was the people in her group who helped her have the courage to work on being honest. She found that every time she did so, she felt a little stronger and more sure of herself.

The biggest part of changing our behaviors has to do with ourselves alone. Grandiosity and resignation are a large part of our disease. For many years we carried voices inside us that said, "I can't do it, I'm not good enough" or, "I can do anything — I don't need help."

For years Bob did his 8 to 5 job and came home to get high every night. Even though he owned the house, he did nothing to help with the upkeep. The few things he would try, he gave up on easily, resigning himself to thinking he could not do it and could not learn how.

Even though Bob was bright, his low self-esteem kept him from believing he could take care of his own house. He also had a history with his father of being severely reprimanded whenever he made a mistake. Several months into his recovery, Bob decided to clean all the storm windows on his house. It was one of those projects he had tried and given up on several times before. For the first time he really heard his voices ("I can't do this . . .") and instead of getting high to drown them out, he spent the day figuring out how to take the windows off and put them back on. Once in a while he felt the urge to give up and quit, but his determination to learn was stronger. At the end of the day he felt an elated sense of accomplishment as well as a deep tiredness. It is hard work and takes a lot of energy to believe in ourselves over the old voices that say we can't.

We all have those voices in one form or another. It is important to remember we are confronting patterns developed over a long time. We will feel stress in our bodies and psyches every time we change or confront those old voices. The more we do it, however, the easier it becomes.

For Mary, who had approached life with the posture, "I'm tough, I can do it myself," it is a new behavior to learn to ask for help, to let other people know she needs them.

It is important to acknowledge the stress of these new behaviors and treat ourselves kindly. Sharing with other people in our group will help remind us we are not alone. This stress is part of becoming a more honest and loving human being.

It is natural to be shaky at first with our changes. This is true of learning anything new in life. Remember riding your first bike?

It is helpful to learn how to reward ourselves for our continuing changes and our desire to grow. In the old days we probably rewarded our accomplishments with our drug. We need to find new ways to reward ourselves — buying ourselves flowers, taking a long bath, going out for dinner at our favorite restaurant.

At the end of Bob's day with the windows, he took himself and his family out for dinner and a movie. For Bob it was a relaxing evening a helpful balance to the struggles of his day.

Learning ways to kindly reward ourselves will help balance out the stress of our new ways. By not expecting too much of ourselves too fast, the stress we encounter will be a natural part of our growth. Remember also that there will be plateaus in our growth, that changes are sometimes so gradual they are hard to notice.

Holidays, Anniversaries:
Those Memory-Laden Times of Year

Let's face it, if we are going to live in the world, we will encounter some situations where alcohol and other drugs will be involved. We will also encounter places, people, and times of year that will trigger memories of painful events, and of our old lifestyle.

Holidays and family gatherings are especially stressful times for most of us. Ellen, who grew up in an alcoholic family, has painful memories around Christmas that go way back. Her own chemical use always escalated around the holidays and she has memories of much tension between herself and the people around her at this time of year.

As a sober adult, the first thing she feels at Christmas is the pain of all those old memories. Then there is the difficulty of finding a new sober way to celebrate. Ellen has been divorced for several years and, though she has been dating, there is no significant man in her life. It is difficult for her to feel good about her sober lifestyle when she is with her father and sisters who still drink. So, for the first time in years, she decides not to travel the distance to see them.

Instead, Ellen spends Christmas Eve with several of her sober women friends. She spends Christmas dinner with a cousin and those of her family with whom she has always felt close. She discovers a more peaceful holiday than she has known for a long time, and yet it is not without its painful moments. This time, however, Ellen has people she can talk to about the pain she is feeling.

There are a lot of expectations about the holidays, and we all feel a certain pressure to fulfill those expectations. There is also the added stress of extra activities this time of year — most of us feel more harried than usual. Let's not forget it is a naturally stressful time and allow ourselves to slow down whenever we possibly can. We can let our holiday be what it needs and wants to be and not try to force moods and events on ourselves and those around us. Each year can be enjoyable in a different way. We can give ourselves permission to be sad, or to enjoy the simple things and quiet times with people we care about.

We are not alone. There are many of us for whom this time of year is difficult. If we find someone to call, it will ease our tension and warm the day for both of us. It is also helpful to plan ahead for our holidays. It will help to know we have a place to go and people to be with at this special time of year.

It is usually more difficult for us to choose not to drink or use other drugs when we find ourselves in situations we have been intoxicated in before. Office parties, weddings, and holidays are a few examples. In Lynn's family, people remember weddings by who got drunk and did the funniest, most outrageous thing. For Lynn to realize how painful her using had become, she could no longer laugh at these historical jokes. She has a large extended family and at family gatherings people begin to avoid her at toast time, or else some forgetful uncle will keep offering her wine.

This is a difficult and painful situation. For Lynn, it brings up her sadness about feeling alone in such a crowd of people who are all family. Lynn is surprised to discover that one of her sisters is in Al-Anon. They begin to mutually support each other at these family gatherings. Lynn also begins to pick and choose which family events she wants to attend.

These kinds of decisions and events are stressful. If we don't have much support in our families, we can take a support person with us. Spouses can be helpful at such times. In any way possible, we should keep in contact with our support system.

Frank found himself feeling somewhat depressed on a warm fall day and he didn't know why. That night at dinner with a friend he realized it was a year ago that fall, on the same kind of day, that his wife left him. As he talked, he remembered how the sun was shining that day, and how angry she was as she left. The more he talked about his own sadness and anger, the less depressed he felt.

We are all affected by anniversaries. It may be a day or a time of year that triggers a painful memory. Sometimes we expect ourselves to just keep going full speed, nonstop, unaffected. It is only human to be affected by such memories. When we talk about them with someone, we treat ourselves kindly. If we fight what we are feeling we only make it harder on ourselves. Let's remember that "this, too, shall pass."

The Interweavings of Change and Stress

Stress charts show that any change affects our level of stress. Moving, getting married, receiving a promotion, a death in the family, a birth, a divorce, or a new relationship all create stress in our lives. Vacation can be stressful and so can the return from vacation. We are creatures of habit, and any change in our routine seems to be stressful. Yet it would be awfully boring to not have any changes, and some studies show that boredom itself is stressful. ("What's wrong with me?", etc.)

Just as pain in our lives is often what pushes us to make major leaps of growth, so does stress stimulate us to grow and change. It is also an integral part of making changes.

It is important to give ourselves time to absorb our changes. The decision to stop using our chemical and look more honestly at ourselves is like a birth and death all rolled into one. We are like young trees needing nourishment and time to grow. The program is the sun and rain that feeds us.

The more patience we have with ourselves, the less tense we will be. If we are having a bad day, maybe we simply need to ease up. We need to learn to take time off, leave work early, or treat ourselves to something we have been wanting to do. If we are worried and there is something we can do about it, we should do it right away. If there is nothing more we can do, we can learn how to let go. Hanging on is stressful and not beneficial to anyone, especially us.

Carl, after a stressful week at work, will often spend a lot of time laying on the couch reading. His wife curls up in bed with a cup of tea and the phone and calls her friends.

We should take time to realize what situations are difficult for us. Is it seeing our family of origin, leading a meeting at work, or dealing with our husband's ex-wife? Whatever it is that is difficult for us, we can learn how to acknowledge it, take time to relax after such encounters, and treat ourselves especially well.

High-Stress Lifestyle As Another Addiction

Just as we once used alcohol or other drugs to numb us to life's realities, it is very possible to use a high-stress lifestyle as an anesthetic. Liz goes from her full-time nursing job to cooking meals for her two daughters and husband, to taking care of her sick mother on weekends. She also likes to volunteer at her children's school. Liz is often edgy and quick to complain about how busy she is. She is not very good at asking her husband for help around the house nor her sisters for help with her mother. Liz prefers to take it all on herself, knowing she is efficient. She has no time to relax with her children and husband and the only time she feels okay about resting more is if she is sick.

Such people are often rewarded by our society. ("That Liz, she's really something, isn't she?") These people often look good, and surely their intentions are good. But we don't do ourselves or anyone else any favors by hiding beneath our busy lives. If we don't take time out for ourselves, we eventually become overloaded. Under her busyness, Liz has not even begun to feel or express her mixed emotions about her father's death a year earlier. She is too busy to feel.

This high-stress lifestyle can be another addiction. Since addiction is a disease of extremes, in this case people go from one crisis to another. In a crisis, feelings and daily life are put aside. A long series of these and people lose touch with their feelings. They keep themselves moving at such an intense speed that no one can feel close to them. The distance between Liz and her family becomes gradually more apparent. This kind of stress exacts a heavy toll on personal relationships and physical health.

Mike is a leading human service worker in a large city and has been instrumental in starting new programs for health care. His intentions and skills are wonderful, but every winter he ends up in the hospital, usually due to exhaustion. His children are showing up in school as behavior problems. His wife is increasingly upset with how little time they have together. Mike has been a definite asset to the community, but his addictive need to continually produce has deeply affected his health and his family life.

When there is no balance between high-stress events and relaxation in our lives, it is possible we are addicted to stress. We must ask ourselves, "Is my lifestyle keeping me from connecting with important people in my life, or keeping me from feeling my own pain? Is my body telling me to slow down?" If so, we will need to find ways to lead a more balanced life, and we may need help doing it.

Letting Go

There is definitely such a thing as too much stress in a person's life. Yet, how do we know when we've reached that point?

It is important to realize that it is different for each of us. The same event may be much more stressful for Carol than it is for her husband, John. On another day, or at a different time in her life, Carol might react differently to the same event. It is important to be aware of what affects us, and to understand that it is different for each individual.

In general, the stress we acquire during events we have no control over can slip us over the line into too much stress pretty easily. During treatment, John talked to his mother about his concerns over her drug usage. Now he continues to worry about her and how she feels about his confrontation. It will be important for John to get clear about what he can do for her and what she will have to do for herself. He needs to choose to let go of what is beyond him, or it will detract from his own sobriety and serenity.

Here is another example of the need to make the same kind of choice. This one is less serious, yet very common in our daily lives. Jean is on her way to meet a friend for coffee and gets held up in traffic. Now, she has a choice. She can escalate her anxiety; she can worry, honk, tighten her muscles, get angry, feel frustrated, etc. All of this will stress her body. Or she can admit she is stuck and realistically see that she's not going to be that late. She could turn on the radio, or make a list in her head of what she needs to do later that day. Traffic eventually does move and she arrives ten minutes late to find her friend reading a book and quite understanding about what happened. Worrying about things beyond us doesn't help ourselves or anyone else. In fact, the stress it puts on us is harmful.

We become overstressed when we deal with stressful situations nonstop. Our bodies are the best monitors of this. Some initial symptoms may include tight body muscles, head or body aches, or an upset stomach. These are often clues that we need to slow down, especially if we have chronic symptoms.

If we don't listen to these clues and continue our lifestyle for a prolonged period of time, the body will collapse in more serious ways. Stress affects the heart as well as other body organs and systems. Too much stress is a significant factor in many illnesses.

It will show up in our relationships when our lives are too busy to be with people who nurture us. Too much stress robs us of quality time and energy to be with our families or close friends. It will also affect our emotions by making us nervous and edgy. When we find ourselves snapping at coworkers, our spouses, and children, we must take some time out.

A prolonged high level of stress will affect us in every area of life. It affects our health, our emotional and spiritual life, and our relationships. When we have crossed the line where stress is no longer conducive to growth we need to do something to ease the pressure.

Finding Balance

Stress management is a term that is fairly common these days. Businesses as well as health care facilities are acknowledging the importance of keeping stress at a manageable level.

Diet and exercise are two important elements of stress management. Eating a proper diet helps keep us well-balanced in our spirits and emotions. Exercise increases our physical strength and endurance, which in turn enables us to handle our lives better. Exercise is also an energizer and a healthy release for frustrations.

Getting enough rest is also important. If, on a day off, the body is longing for a nap, listen to it. Our bodies are very wise — the more we listen to them and honor them, the better we will feel.

Learning to talk about painful situations in our lives will help. The A.A. program is an invaluable asset, for we are given a place to go to talk and listen to others. Many of us did not have such an outlet before we found the program.

Let's not underestimate the power of sharing our problems. We will feel lighter and less burdened when we are not alone with our pain.

We can learn what it is that relaxes us and take time to do it. In the middle of the day, we should consciously relax our muscles until we feel the release of tension. We might try some form of meditation. Meditation is really a focused concentration on any single activity. Some people do it running, others drawing. There are many ways to achieve the serenity of being entirely focused on one thing.

Let's try different things and find out what works for us. Is it a hot bath, a long walk, a good book, a nap? Whatever works, we have our permission and encouragement to do it.

We may need to organize our time and set priorities. If we continually overschedule ourselves, we must learn how to let go of the bottom of our list of priorities and forgive ourselves if we don't get everything done. Life is not a race to see who can pack the most into a day. As recovering human beings, we tend to be hard on ourselves. We need some time every day for relaxation and pleasure.

Again and again, it will be to our advantage to learn how to let go of worrying about things we can do nothing about. Part of the wisdom of the Zen philosophy is learning to observe something, feel it, then let it go.

This is much of what the Twelve Steps are about. For most of us, letting go is difficult, but we can do it. We can take deep breaths and accept when something is beyond our control. We will be saving ourselves a lot of unproductive tension. We all have something to learn from the wisdom of letting go — it is worth working at. The stress we carry concerning events we can do nothing about eats away at our spirits and bodies.

Laughter and play are important tension-releasers. There is a humorous side to even our most serious problems. We need to learn to incorporate play and relaxation into our daily lives — they are an important counterpart to the natural stress of life.

It is also important to learn our limitations. How many nights a week do we need at home to maintain our sanity? How many meetings do we need at this time in our lives? When we feel our serenity bulging at its seams, let's acknowledge that we are stretching our limits.

The more we learn to say no at this point, the healthier we will be. For many of us, learning to say no and admitting, even to ourselves, that we have limits is a new behavior. We most likely need a lot of support to do so and not feel guilty. Our serenity is well worth learning to say no for, when we need to.

All of these are ways to manage the stress of life. We must first learn our warning signals. Then we must begin to say no, to slow down, and take time out. As preventive medicine we can build play and relaxation into our lives. We can recognize the special stress factors we encounter as recovering human beings, as well as the common factors any human being encounters. The slogans of the program were created for good reason. "Keep it simple," "Easy does it," "A day at a time." It really does help to apply these daily to our lives.

Remember the analogy that stress is like the tension on a violin string. We will always need "enough to make music, but not so much that it snaps." Part of recovering is continuing to examine and learn what that delicate balance is in each of our lives.

The stress that is a part of our growth, and the growth itself, is the music of our lives. We must celebrate our growth and keep learning how to let go of the stress that may snap and rob us of our own music.

The music that is us is made up of our bodies, our health, our relationships, our spiritual lives, and our growing changes. Above all, we deserve to enjoy life. We can embrace the sorrow and the joy. Like any good piece of music, life is a composition of both.

Hazelden, a national nonprofit organization founded in 1949, helps people reclaim their lives from the disease of addiction. Built on decades of knowledge and experience, Hazelden offers a comprehensive approach to addiction that addresses the full range of patient, family, and professional needs, including treatment and continuing care for youth and adults, research, higher learning, public education and advocacy, and publishing.

A life of recovery is lived "one day at a time." Hazelden publications, both educational and inspirational, support and strengthen lifelong recovery. In 1954, Hazelden published *Twenty-Four Hours a Day*, the first daily meditation book for recovering alcoholics, and Hazelden continues to publish works to inspire and guide individuals in treatment and recovery, and their loved ones. Professionals who work to prevent and treat addiction also turn to Hazelden for evidence-based curricula, informational materials, and videos for use in schools, treatment programs, and correctional programs.

Through published works, Hazelden extends the reach of hope, encouragement, help, and support to individuals, families, and communities affected by addiction and related issues.

For questions about Hazelden publications, please call **800-328-9000** or visit us online at **hazelden.org/bookstore**.